Cryptocurrency wallets

Table of Contents

Chapter 1: Introduction
- 1.1. What is a cryptocurrency wallet?
- 1.2. How cryptocurrency wallets work
- 1.3. Relationship between Private key, Public key and cryptocurrency wallet addresses
- 1.4. Differences between cryptocurrency wallets and an exchange
- 1.5. Types of cryptocurrency wallets

Chapter 2: Desktop wallets (software wallets)
- 2.1. Exodus
- 2.2. Copay
- 2.3. Armory wallet
- 2.4. Electrum
- 2.5. Etherwall

Chapter 3: Mobile wallets
- 3.1. Coinomi
- 3.2. Enjin
- 3.3. Bread wallet
- 3.4. Jaxx
- 3.5. imToken

Chapter 4: Web wallets
- 4.1. GreenAddress
- 4.2. BitGo
- 4.3. Blockchain.info
- 4.4. MyEtherWallet
- 4.5. MetaMask

Chapter 5: Hardware wallets
- 5.1. Trezor
- 5.2. Ledger Nano S

Chapter 6: Paper wallets
Conclusion
Acknowledgement

Chapter 1: Introduction

For one to hold cryptocurrencies, they need to have a special storage for these digital currencies. Normal currencies are stored either in banks or are held as liquid cash. To keep money in a bank, one needs to have a unique account number, which is issued by the bank. One can share his or her account number with people wishing to send money to him. One can transfer money from his or her account to another person's account. Lastly, one can choose to withdraw the money held in the account and store it in a leather wallet. All operations done with a bank account are monitored and regulated by the bank. When there are suspicious transactions, the bank can choose to suspend the holder's account. However, when one withdraws money and keeps it in a wallet, the regulations and monitoring cease. One has absolute control over the wallet. The concept of a cryptocurrency wallet is not much different from this.

1.1. What is a cryptocurrency wallet?

A cryptocurrency wallet is a digital wallet used for storing, sending, receiving and tracking digital currency holdings; both cryptocurrencies and tokens. Cryptocurrency wallets combine the advantages of a physical wallet with the convenience, flexibility, and sophistication of a digital platform. A single wallet can keep different digital currencies but there are some wallets that have restrictions on the coins that they accept. Therefore, Bitcoin, Ethereum, and Monero can be stored in the same wallet. A wallet will package them in different sections for the convenience of checking balances or doing transactions. Cryptocurrency wallets come with balance checkers and these keep users informed of the cryptocurrencies that they currently hold. For one to own any cryptocurrency, he or she must have these wallets. However, it is important to familiarize ourselves with how they work.

1.2. How cryptocurrency wallets work

Cryptocurrency wallets can be likened to safety deposit boxes that financial institutions rent out to people to keep their valuables such as jewelry, bonds, and sensitive documents. The person that has rented the deposit box is normally given a key or some other type of security pass to access the box. Institutions that rent out these boxes emphasize on the owners keeping tabs on where their keys are at all times. This is because the loss of a key could easily translate to the loss of everything stored in the safety deposit box.

Cryptocurrency wallets use the same concepts. Cryptocurrencies are not actually stored in a crypto wallet, instead, only private and Public keys are stored in the wallet. This is because cryptocurrencies do not have any physical form of existence thus cannot be stored in a given location the same way money can be. All that determines that one owns a cryptocurrency are records stored by the blockchain. To better familiarize ourselves with this, let us learn more about the keys stored by a cryptocurrency wallet and how they show ownership of cryptocurrencies. A Private key is a special hexadecimal code that is only known by the owner and the wallet. The Private key shows that one is the owner of a certain Public key and the Public key is what is connected to the amount of cryptocurrency that one holds. Private keys can be and are regularly stolen especially through cyber attacks. When a Private key is stolen, the hacker will simply import the address to their own wallet and then move the cryptocurrencies to another wallet. This is because the Private key is mathematically related to a Private key and the person that holds the Private key is the rightful owner of the

...nds connected to the related Public key. Wallet addresses. A Private key looks much like this:

```
3831556b5fe7ffg8g57cdd296dc3g22g3b9cggdef6529267b9d1a44aa137558
```

It is obvious that keeping such a key as a form of ownership of a particular cryptocurrency is a daunting task. This is why wallets exist, they store such keys in a more convenient way. However, out of precaution, cryptocurrency holders are always advised to have a safer backup option for their Private key. In case something was to happen to the wallet that they used to keep the Private keys, they would still be able to import these Private keys to another wallet and not lose any of their funds. Private keys are necessary in that they are the only acceptable authorizations to allow one to access their cryptocurrencies or to make transfers.

1.3. Relationship between Private key, Public key and cryptocurrency wallet addresses

As we have mentioned before, the two important keys that will be generated when you create a wallet are the Private and the Public key. To receive funds, you will need a wallet address. Both the Private key and the Public key are large integer numbers, but since these numbers are so large, they are usually represented using a separate Wallet Import Format (WIF) consisting of letters and numbers.

To begin with, the Private key can be generated in different ways depending on the wallet. Some wallet will tell you to type a phrase, others will generate phrases for you and others will tell you to move your cursor around your computer screen. Once you have done that, they will mostly use elliptical curve cryptography to generate the Private key. The Private key is any point in the curve generated using your seed or phrase. This is the sensitive key since if it is revealed to anyone else, it can be used by the person to recover all your funds.

The Public key is derived from the Private key using a mathematical function. The Public key can easily be generated from the Private key. However, it is very difficult to derive the Private key from the Public key. The Public key is therefore not a major concern even if it is viewed by other people. It cannot be used to recover your Private key. If one was to attempt to recover the Private key, it could take them lots of computing power that is currently unavailable or millions of years of trials.

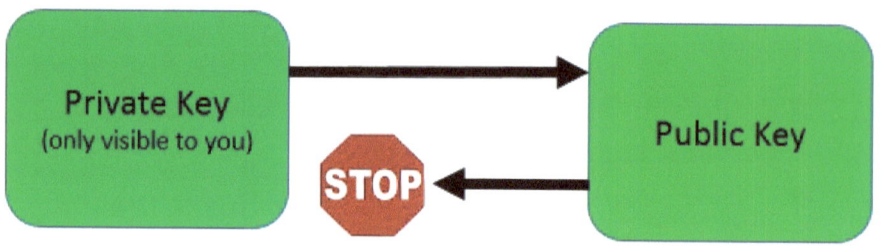

To receive funds, wallets will use an address, just the way you have an account number. The wallet address is derived from the Public key. It is a hash of the Public key. This means that, your wallet takes your Private key and passes it through a hashing algorithm to derive a wallet address. You can have very many wallet addresses. For Bitcoin, one can use a new address for every transaction.

Cryptocurrency wallet addresses are mathematically related to the Public key. A Public key is 256 bits long and when hashed and concatenated, a 160 bits long address is formed. The 160 bits long address is the wallet address. Therefore, the Private key is mathematically related to the Public key which is mathematically related to the wallet address. For security purposes, it is extremely difficult to find the Private key if one has a Public key. The exchange of cryptocurrencies is done via the wallet addresses.

1.4. Differences between cryptocurrency wallets and an exchange

Exchanges are essentially platforms on which one can change from one cryptocurrency to another. For instance, if a Bitcoin owner sees that Bitcoin is not gaining value as fast as Ethereum is, he or she will go to an exchange to convert Bitcoin coins to Ethereum. Wallets are not capable of doing such conversion. The exchange can be understood as a Forex Bureau. When one wishes to change from US dollars to Yen they can only do so at the foreign exchange bureau.

The confusing bit is that many exchanges allow users to store cryptocurrency in them. However, there are stack differences between a wallet and an exchange even if it stores cryptocurrencies. To begin with, a wallet is personal but an exchange is owned by another party. Even though an exchange such as coinbase will tell users that they can use the coinbase wallet, the user will not be in direct ownership of the cryptocurrencies in the exchange. Therefore, if Bob has X amount of Bitcoin in Coinbase, Bob does not directly have custody of the coins. If anything bad was to happen and Coinbase was to disappear, Bob would lose all his Bitcoin stored by Coinbase.

It is always advisable to only keep money in an exchange when necessary. In most other incidents, they should remain in one's custody. There is a very good reason behind this, hacking. Many cryptocurrency exchanges are hacked. When they are hacked, users that had stored cryptocurrencies in the exchanges end up at a loss as they lose everything. Cryptocurrencies do not leave as many digital trails as normal currencies. Therefore, when such a loss happens, chances of recovery are very slim. By early 2018, up to 980,000 Bitcoin had been stolen by hackers from cryptocurrency exchanges. Unfortunately, due to lack of regulation of cryptocurrencies, the monies lost is not compensated and neither is the exchange legally required to compensate its users. Big exchanges such as Coincheck, Bitgrail, and Coinrail have all been hacked and some of the users that had stored cryptocurrencies on these exchanges lost them.

Therefore, a wallet only allows the storage and spending of cryptocurrencies while an exchange allows a digital coin to be converted to another coin or fiat currency. Even though exchanges allow users to store cryptocurrencies on them, they should not be used as the ultimate solutions to wallets. The exchanges are not liable for any losses a user might incur when their ryptocurrencies are stolen. Wallets are much more secure since the user will hold Private key. Even if a certain wallet disappears, the holder of the ryptocurrencies will simply switch to another wallet and move the ryptocurrencies there. Lastly, exchanges have some withdrawal limits. This is because they are cryptocurrency traders. They can, therefore, put some restrictions as to how many coins of a certain cryptocurrency that one can withdraw.

1.5. Types of cryptocurrency wallets

There are different types of cryptocurrency. The wallets depend on the medium that they are stored. Therefore, there can be hardware, software, desktop and paper wallets. In addition to this, there is a categorization of hot and cold wallets depending on whether the wallet is online or offline. The following is a summarized explanation of each type of wallet.

- Desktop wallets - Desktop wallets are cryptocurrency wallets installed on personal computers or laptops.
- Mobile wallets – these are cryptocurrency wallets that run as apps on phones
- Hardware wallets – these are special hardware that can be connected to computers and are designed to specifically hold Private keys and keep them secure.
- Paper wallet – there is normally an option to print out QR codes of private and Public keys of cryptocurrencies. When these are printed on a paper or the keys written on the paper, the paper becomes a paper wallet.

- Web wallet – this is a web-based wallet. It is not downloaded to a local computer, rather, it is hosted on a real or virtual server accessible from the internet.

In addition, you should take note of the following categorizations of wallets:

- Hot wallets – this is a categorization of all wallets that are connected to the internet or are online
- Cold wallets – this is a categorization of all wallets that are offline

Chapter 2: Desktop wallets (software wallets)

Desktop wallets are software applications downloaded and installed on one's computer. The wallet will only be accessible on the computer that it was installed on. Therefore, if one travels and leaves behind the computer that they installed their desktop wallets, they will not be able to access the wallet till they physically get back to the computer. Desktop wallets are hailed to have some of the highest levels of security. This is because they are only accessible by the user of the computer and no one else. They are also comparatively more difficult to steal from than mobile wallets. The biggest challenge with these is that, if the computer in which the wallet is kept was to be hacked or infected with malware, there is a high chance that one could lose all the funds stored in it. Global cyber attacks such as the 2016 WannaCry ransomware that encrypted computers in over 150 countries are some of the security scares for people that prefer to keep their funds on desktop wallets. The following is an evaluation of the pros and cons of desktop wallets:

Pros

- Control – desktop wallets offer a user full access to both the public and Private keys as well as the seed. These can be used to restore the wallet if necessary. Also, they also allow for user-controlled security to protect these from being stolen or lost.
- Additional security products – desktop wallets are more secured from threats such as viruses than mobile wallets because there are many effective cyber security products developed for desktops. A desktop can have an antivirus program, host-based firewall, host-based intrusion prevention system and full disk encryption. Therefore, malware are prevented from infecting it, the firewall keeps malicious traffic at bay, the IPS prevents potentially harmful activities such as port scanning on the computer and full disk encryption ensures that the computer's contents cannot be accessed by hackers even if they succeed at stealing the computer or its hard disk.
- Multiple backup options – there are many free backup solutions developed for computers and these could come in handy when backing up the sensitive files from the desktop. Backing up these files ensures that, even if something unfortunate such as virus infection happens on the computer, the user can still install the same wallet on a different computer and recover all the necessary data without losing any funds in the process.
- Ability to switch to cold storage – the owner of the cryptocurrencies can decide to install the desktop wallet on a rarely used computer and then disconnect it from the internet. With this,

the wallet will be a cold wallet which is essentially safer than hot wallets, that is, wallets connected to the internet.

Cons

- Hacking – hackers are targeting computers and specifically the folders known to keep wallet files containing sensitive data such as Private keys. Even though there may be more security products for computers, they are costly and thus most users will be running basic versions of antivirus programs that do not offer an all-rounded protection. There are more threats against desktop computers as well, some of which strike using zero-day exploits that are not known by antivirus programs. Therefore, hacking will always be a significant threat to desktop wallets.
- Hard disk crash – it is not unheard off for a perfectly functioning computer to experience a hard disk crash. When this happens, the disk may be corrupted hence all the data stored inside may be lost. If the desktop wallet on the hard disk was not backed up, the owner might lose all funds stored in the wallet.
- Blockchain update – a desktop wallet must be connected to the internet to download the whole Blockchain each time one wants to make a transaction. There are locations with poor internet connections. There are computers that have limited storage. These issues may make the desktop wallet unusable.
- Usage – even though there has not been a widespread adoption of cryptocurrencies by major businesses, the world is headed there. With online and mobile wallets, it is easy for a cryptocurrencies

owner to pay for items on the go using these wallets. However, it is not so feasible for someone to carry around his or her laptop or desktop just to be able to use it at payment points factoring in that the laptop will have to also download and sync the Blockchain before the payment can be done.

Having looked at the pros and cons of desktop wallets, you are able to judge its suitability. We can now look at the types of desktop wallets in the market today. These are as follows:

2.1. Exodus

Figure 1: Exodus user interface

This is one of the most recognized names in the wallet market. It is the first desktop wallet to come with inbuilt ShapeShift in its interface. ShapeShift is a revolutionary and easy to use cryptocurrency exchange platform. The integration of ShapeShift in Exodus allows a user to instantly change their cryptocurrencies without having to leave the Exodus interface. As said before, cryptocurrency exchanges are insecure locations to keep funds but in this setup, the funds will remain in the custody of the owner since they will be held by Exodus and not the exchange platform.

Reviewers rate Exodus highly since it has a simplified, aesthetic and easy to learn interface. The interface also gives users access to many functionalities and it is, therefore, a preferred wallet by crypto-traders. Exodus is also a multicurrency wallet meaning that it can be used to store different coins in the same wallet. As of 2018, the wallet supported over 110 coins. The coins that the wallet supports are what enable the instantaneous ShapeShift exchange transactions to take place. It is, therefore, a very useful tool for cryptocurrency investors and traders that keep switching between cryptocurrencies. The wallet comes with a backup wizard that simplifies and secures the backup procedure for users.

There are only three cons of Exodus. It is not multi-signature and does not have 2-factor authentication thus its security levels are not optimal considering the increased cyber security threats. The platform is also only partially open source. The issue with this is that the wallet does not enjoy the open source community benefits of getting reviewed and updated faster depending on the feedback of many people in the community. Nevertheless, it is a very good wallet and one that has very many users.

2.2. Copay

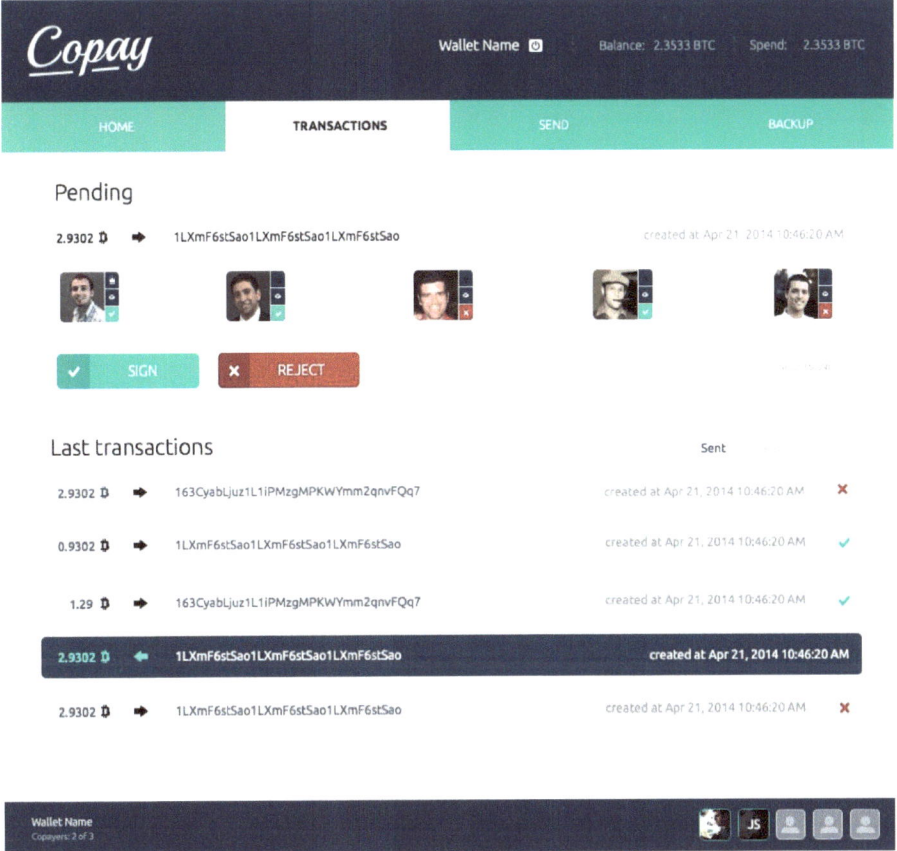

Figure 2: Copay wallet interface

This is primarily a Bitcoin wallet that is developed by BitPay, a Bitcoin payment service provider. BitPay designed this wallet to give Bitcoin owners a convenient, secure and optimized platform to keep their money. Copay features state-of-the-art security features and high levels of transparency that makes it the wallet of choice for many Bitcoin enthusiasts. Copay features multi-sig (multisignature) which is a security feature requiring more than one user to authorize a transaction. Therefore, the user can set up another party to sign a transaction in order for it to take place. The advantage of this is that it becomes very hard for a malicious person to steal Bitcoin from a user that has a Copay wallet. Even if the intruder knows the user's key, it is impossible to finalize a transaction using that key only. The wallet is also optimized for sharing. For instance, a partnership business could store a shared Copay wallet with complete trust that none of the partners will be able to withdraw the money without the authorization of other partners.

Another advantage of Copay is the ease of backup and recovery. Since the wallet is a hierarchical deterministic one, backup files can be used to automatically restore funds that were in a wallet before it was deleted, corrupted or lost. Copay also offers remote backup storage thus users' needs of having a secure backup location have already been met. Since the wallet is open source, it enjoys contributions from the open source community aimed at making it better and even more secure. Its close links with one of the leading Bitcoin payment merchant says a lot about the applicability of the wallet. Copay is also multiplatform, it is available for desktops and smartphones. It is a convergence of security and convenience. A user can seamlessly access the same wallet on either their smartphone or computer. Copay is one of the few wallets that support this multiplatform user environment. One of the main cons of this wallet is the lack of 2-factor authentication. This means that, if a hacker manages to steal or guess the wallet's password, they will get direct access to the money stored therein. Copay, however, makes up for this with multi-sig as has been explained.

2.3. Armory wallet

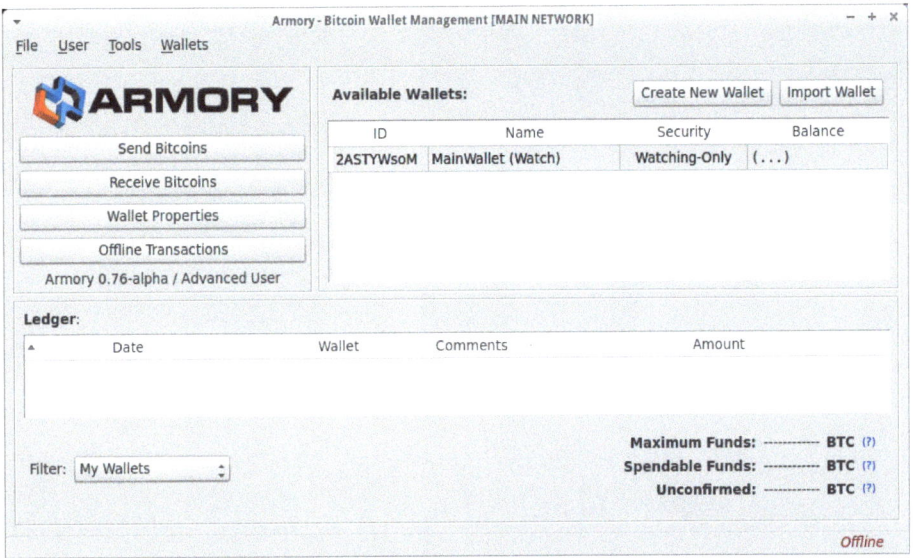

Figure 3: Armory wallet interface

This is a distinctive desktop wallet that has won the hearts of users that prefer cold storage for their coins. Cold storage gives a higher level of security since it does not expose the funds to threats all over the internet. With the increase in crypto malware attacks, users that own many coins prefer keeping them in cold storage. Armory is commonly used by the more experienced users in the cryptocurrency world. It is the only open source yet cold storage wallet which means that it is not owned by an individual or an organization, rather, it is from the open source community and regularly gets performance and security contributions from it. This has already come in handy in that the original developer company already stopped working on it but just one developer with the help of the open source community has kept it going since then. The wallet supports multisignature support which is an added layer of security to prevent unauthorized people from successfully making transactions even if they breach a user's wallet. A combination of these features makes armory a good choice for security-conscious users since it offers cold storage, multi-sig and open source support in one package.

    Armory is praised to be the safest Bitcoin wallet due to its advanced security features. It gives its users a peace of mind by keeping their coins in the most secure location. Cold storage is the safest option for any cryptocurrency. Even exchanges move their cryptocurrencies to cold storage wallets when they are not trading them just to be sure that they cannot be accessed by anyone. The main issue with this wallet is the uncertainty of its future. With all but one of the original developers abandoning it, there are serious concerns about its stability and performance going forward.

2.4. Electrum

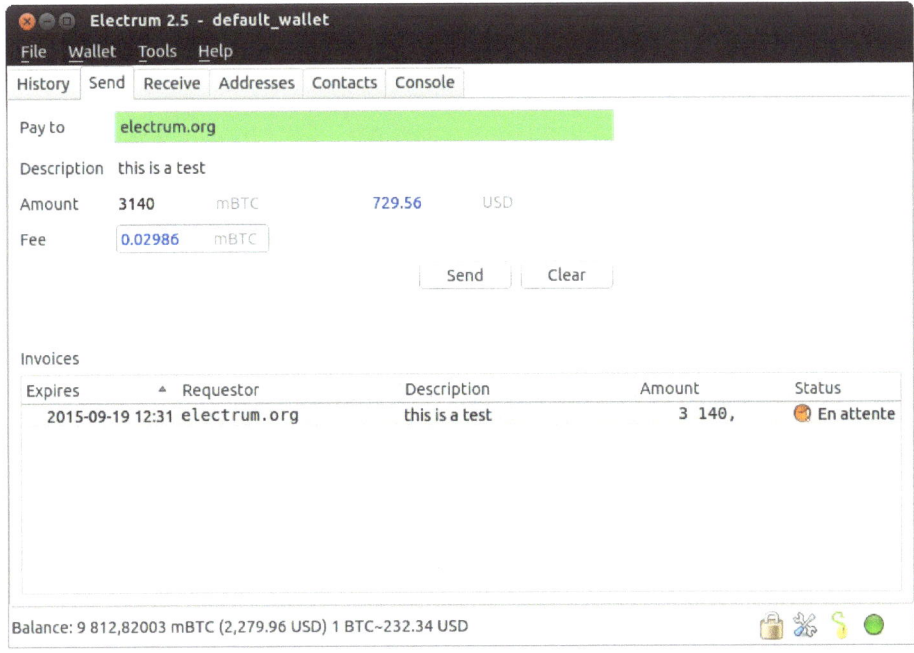

Figure 4: Electrum wallet on Linux

It's a wallet that was released in 2011 after a lengthy development period by developers who wanted it to be the most robust and efficient wallet. It is amongst the earliest entrants into the market, at a time when Bitcoin was worth a few dollars. It has not lost its glory as it is estimated that 10% of all Bitcoins are transacted through this wallet. The wallet supports Windows, Mac and Linux. In addition, it has a mobile version as well. The wallet is open source thus is not built on proprietary languages and has seen contributions from many developers in the open source community over the years. Electrum is only focused on Bitcoin despite there being very many altcoins. This sole focus ensures that the wallet is fast and efficient for all Bitcoin users. Electrum runs as a Bitcoin client and the advantage of this is that it directly interface with the Bitcoin network. Unlike other wallets, it, therefore, does not need to download the Blockchain in order to be able to run transactions as it is already interfaced with Bitcoin.

Another key feature of this wallet is that it easily integrates with major hardware wallets. Electrum is recognized as one of the most secure Bitcoin wallets. This is because it has strong encryption algorithms used to secure Private keys such that a hacker cannot retrieve them even if they breach a user's computer. The wallet also has a reliable and secure seed that is used to generate Private keys. The security of the seed is said to be similar to that used by Bitcoin itself. The seed is used to recover passwords thus its security is of utmost importance since if it is accessed by a hacker can use it to reset passwords and steal cryptocurrencies from one's wallet. In addition to this, Electrum has 2-factor authentication and multi-sig, a combination that makes this wallet impervious to hackers or unauthorized money transfers. The only major con, that has already been fixed, is that there was a time when Electrum users were losing funds. It came to be observed that this happened if they were logged into their Electrum wallets and visited some infected websites that had been overrun by hackers. However, this was quickly patched and the wallet has never seen any other security flaw.

2.5. Etherwall

As the name suggests, this is an Ethereum wallet. The wallet is commonly used by Ethereum enthusiasts. It is open source and can run in two modes. The first mode is where it runs as a full node client. This means that the wallet regularly downloads the entire Ethereum Blockchain. The second mode that it can run in is the thin client mode. In this mode, the wallet just directly interfaces with he Ethereum network thus there is no longer the need to download the Blockchain. When interfaced, it will use a remote node for data retrieval and also for sending transactions. Etherwall is built for Windows, Mac, and Linux.

There, however, are many concerns about this wallet. The first issue is that the wallet is not hierarchical deterministic thus backups cannot be used to restore funds that were in the wallet in case the computer on which it was installed crashes, is infected with viruses or is formatted. Another concern is that the wallet is hardly secure. The wallet does not have multi-sig, therefore, if a hacker gains access to the wallet, they can simply make transactions without any barriers. The other security concern is that the wallet does not have 2-factor authentication. If a hacker is able to guess or steal a user's password, they can steal the funds in the wallet. With the current security fears due to increased cyber breaches on personal computers leading to the theft of cryptocurrencies, these are major concerns. Etherwall does not have a clean history as well. There have been several cases of users losing their Ethereum after their Private keys are stolen possibly through phishing.

Nevertheless, Etherwall is easily integrated with Trezor which is a hardware wallet. Therefore, for increased security, users can easily transfer their funds to the cold storage Trezor wallet. This helps to settle some of the security fears that users might have.

Chapter 3: Mobile wallets

Mobile wallets are built with the convenience of making payments in mind. Desktop wallets are efficient in matters of security but they are almost unusable while on the go such as when one wants to make payments at a store. Many desktop wallets have been making mobile variants to tap into the consumer market of users that just want a convenient wallet that they can carry around wherever they go. Mobile wallets run as apps on smartphones. The following are some of the widely used mobile wallets:

3.1. Coinomi

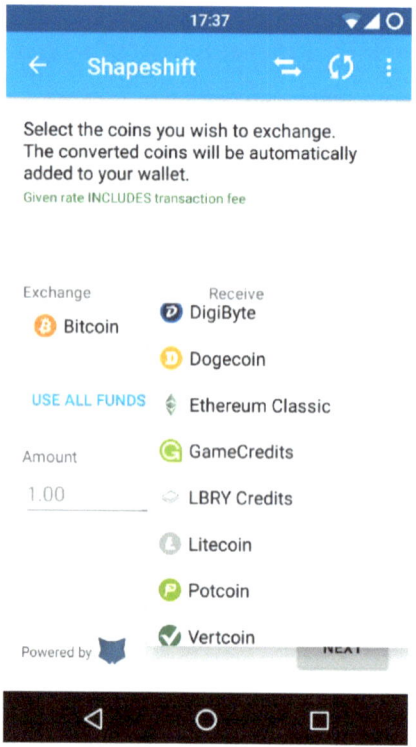

Figure 5: Coinomi interface showing inbuilt ShapeShift

Coinomi is one of the most used mobile wallets that is available to both Android and iOS users. Coinomi is strictly a mobile app thus does not have an online or desktop variant. It supports over 20 commonly used cryptocurrencies which are just about enough for those wishing to make transactions in cryptocurrency form. Moreover, the wallet keeps on adding support to many other coins over time and is also supporting tokens. Coinomi is said to be secure within the standards of a mobile app. The wallet will generate a new address for each transaction using a secured seed. If one loses the app or their phone, they can still use the seed to recreate everything. Coinomi says that a user's Private key never leaves the device thus is not at risk of being intercepted by hackers. The wallet is also anonymous and it hides the user's IP address, does not do any tracking and has servers whose focus is to anonymize transactions. The level of privacy that Coinomi offers is unmatched by other mobile wallets.

In terms of convenience, this wallet sets the bar high up for other mobile wallets. Coinomi comes with ShapeShift and Changelly integrated with the app. These two are recognized crypto exchanges in the market. Therefore a user can quickly and easily convert between several coins without ever having to move funds from his or her wallet. Coinomi also leverages these exchange platforms to enable cross-chain transfers. Cross chain transfers are those involving alt coins and Bitcoin. Coinomi is built for an international user market thus supports very many languages. It also goes the extra step of showing users their balances in different coins just in case one would wish to quickly convert the coins.

The main disadvantage with this wallet comes as a necessary evil for the type of privacy features that the wallet has. If one was to lose their wallet password and forget their seed phrase, they would consequently lose all their funds stored in this wallet. This is because Coinomi does not have a centralized store for passwords and Private keys. It is, therefore, the user's responsibility to keep these two pieces of data safe elsewhere just in case they lose their phone. Another disadvantage to keep in mind is that there have been controversies that Coinomi has ever been hacked even though the company denies it. A user said that there is a time that their app started to transmit their Bitcoin addresses to another IP address indicating that the app had been hacked. If these allegations are true, the wallet is therefore not spotless in terms of falling victim to hacking.

3.2. Enjin

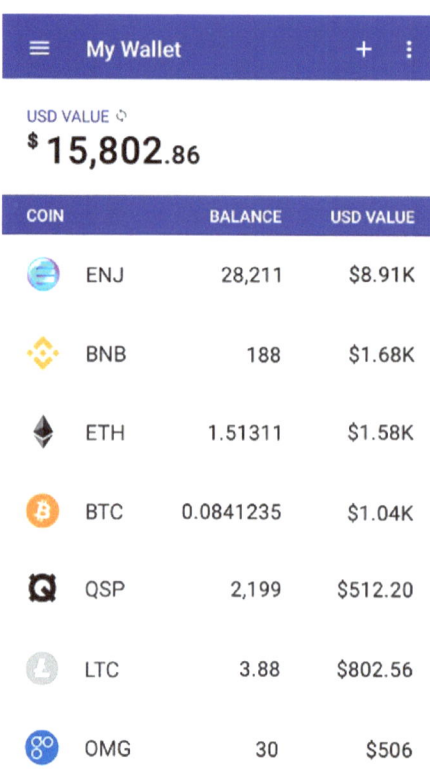

Figure 6: Enjin wallet app

There are wallets that keep pushing security standards further and Enjin is one of them. Despite being a hot wallet, it is an advanced wallet that can make a smartphone to reach security levels only achievable in a hardware wallet. There is no doubt that it is among the most secured wallets. To seal any loopholes in the security of the app, developers have created a custom keyboard that appears during the entry of passwords. This prevents the use of third-party apps, some of which could contain scripts to copy inputs from a user and send them to a hacker. The keyboard is also randomized. Therefore, keys are not arranged in any standard format. This makes it hard for any keylogger or shoulder surfer to tell what is being typed. Shoulder surfers are malicious people that steal login credentials by staring at the users' screens or keyboards during the input process.

Also in line with the strict security measures in the app, the 12-character seed that the app uses for each user cannot be copied. This is to prevent it from being stored in the clipboard or temporarily in the RAM where malware can access it. The seed is only shown on the screen but the user cannot save or copy it. It is also encrypted with a password that the user sets. This password is also protected from being copied and neither does the input field allow pasting of values. Further, one cannot take screenshots in the app nor use apps meant to record videos on the screen. During its operation, the wallet claims to have RAM encryption. This is to protect it from the group of vulnerabilities known as Spectre and Meltdown that have been said to be present in almost all computer chips. These flaws were introduced in chips to help computers work faster through aggressive speculative execution and caching. These vulnerabilities can essentially be used to retrieve sensitive data during a program's execution even without privileges to do so.

Another feature that makes Enjin a highly sought after wallet is its support for ERC-20 protocol. Users can, therefore, receive and store tokens obtained from ICOs in this wallet. Needless to say, this is one of the most water-tight security standards for any wallet. Enjin operates on a security level of its own which is unmatched. If one loses their phone with Enjin, they are sure that their coins or tokens are secure. The app is free and does not show ads for revenue generation purposes. Enjin has its own ERC-20 coin that is gaining value with the increased adoption of the app. The app has a simplified interface despite the rather complex backend. It also shows a user's balance in fiat currency such as USD.

The only limitation with this wallet is that it currently only works with Android but the developers are working on an iOS version. Another concern is that the app is not open source and it is obviously due to security reasons. It is, however, a security fear for users worried about transparency and privacy since they inherently have to trust that the developers have not added malicious lines of codes to steal from the users or collect sensitive information about the users.

3.3. Bread wallet

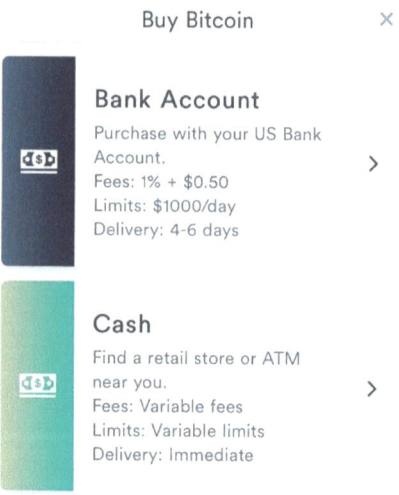

Figure 7: Bread wallet app

This is a wallet that is built with simplicity and minimalism in mind. It supports a limited number of cryptocurrencies. These are Bitcoin, Bitcoin Cash, Ethereum, and ERC-20 compliant tokens. Bread is highly renowned for its human-centered design, it is arguably the easiest wallet for a beginner in cryptocurrency to get started with. It is intuitive and straight-forward thus simplifying many things for anyone new in cryptocurrencies. The app is currently available for iOS and Android apps. It is free to download but cryptocurrency transactions will be charged. The wallet is linked to one's bank and transaction fees get charged to the bank instead of being included in the cryptocurrencies being transacted. This is part of the reason why it is ideal for new users.

To set up a bread wallet is quite easy. A new user will be asked to set up a 6-character password to be used every time they want to log into the wallet. They are then given a 12-word seed that they have to write on a paper. This is what they can use to recover the wallet in the cases of theft, disappearance or technical issues with the phone. Just to check whether the user has written down the seed, the app asks the user to re-enter the words.

After the confirmation, all is done and the wallet is all set up. One can transfer their cryptocurrencies to the wallet through the receive menu. However, since it is meant to be a beginner's wallet, Bread allows users to buy coins via the app or gives them a map of where they can buy coins in cash through Bitcoin ATMs or verified local sellers. Since app partners with third-party payment services, one can also purchase the coins directly on the app and pay with their banks. Ideally, the wallet cuts the separation of fiat currency and cryptocurrency by integrating both worlds in the same app. A user will not be forced to purchase cryptocurrencies from exchanges, they will be able to buy whilst on the app.

Bitcoin is built to be secure in that it does not send a user's information back and forth to its servers and then the cryptocurrency network. Instead, it interfaces directly with the crypto network allowing for direct and decentralized handling of transactions. The app does not store the user's Private keys as well thus there are fewer vulnerabilities that target it. The only sensitive information is the seed which is highly secured and only the user is supposed to know it. The cons of this wallet are that it does not support multi-sig and 2-factor authentication. These are great additions to a wallet that give an additional layer of security from hackers. Other than this, Bread is a highly recommendable wallet for beginners.

3.4. Jaxx

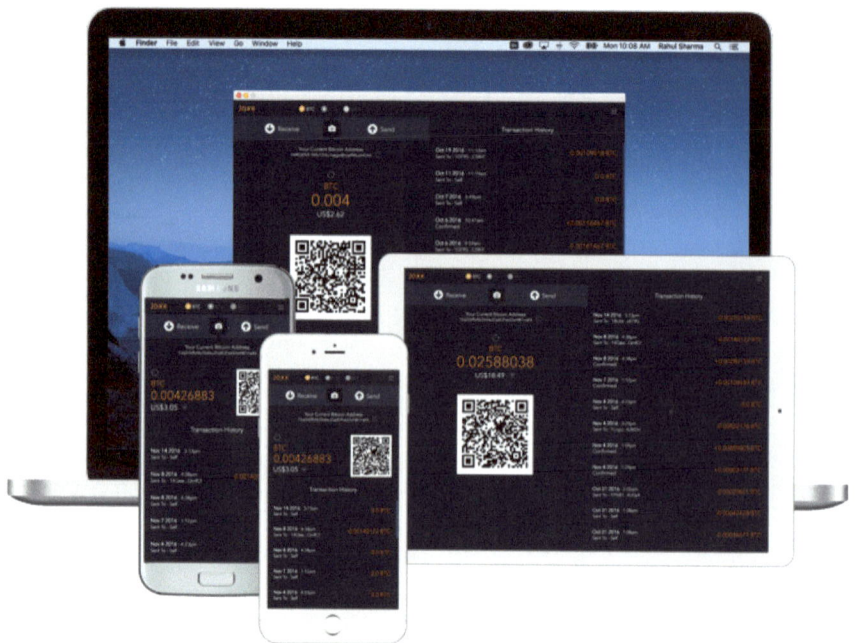

Figure 8: The entire suite of Jaxx platforms

Jaxx is a commonly used wallet due to the fact that it is multiplatform. It supports iOS, Android, Windows, Mac, Linux and also has Chrome and Firefox extensions for web-based use. This sets it apart from many wallets. In addition to this, Jaxx is among the wallets that support very many cryptocurrencies and tokens. Over 60 crypto assets can be held in Jaxx. Jaxx was built with a goal of attracting the masses. This goal seems to have been met due to the many platforms it is accessible from and the number of cryptocurrencies it supports. Jaxx has also been built with an aesthetic and easy to use interface that many of its users find to be quite friendly. Since it is accessible from many platforms, Jaxx has a feature called cross-platform pairing. This enables the same wallet to be accessed across different devices, the same way one would access their Gmail accounts over a number of platforms. The wallet is free and makes money through ShapeShift transactions. The wallets come with an inbuilt ShapeShift module that allows for the quick and direct conversion between coins without the user having to leave the wallet.

In addition to holding over 60 cryptocurrencies and tokens, Jaxx also allows users to store their fiat currencies in it just as they would store in their bank accounts. Therefore, one can safely store fiat currency directly on Jaxx and make payments or receive more funds through the same wallet. Jaxx is also anonymous and does not collect user information during sign up. All the keys created by the wallet are safely stored on the user's device and are not transmitted. It is the user's responsibility to ensure that these keys, however, do not get discovered by other people. A Jaxx account is normally backed up through a master seed. This seed can help a user recover their funds just in case the device on which they were running their wallet on is stolen or is lost.

The biggest issue with this wallet is the performance. Since the wallet supports so many cryptocurrencies, it takes it a long time to start up and load all of them. Mobile users have to wait for about 15 seconds for this process to take place. Also, transactions through the app's inbuilt ShapeShift also take some time. Users have complained that at times, their transactions fail to register forcing them to repeatedly try carrying them out again.

Despite the listed concerns, Jaxx is a fairly good all-in-one package. Not only does it support very many cryptocurrencies, it is accessible over very many platforms. It has a user-friendly interface and enough security.

3.5. imToken

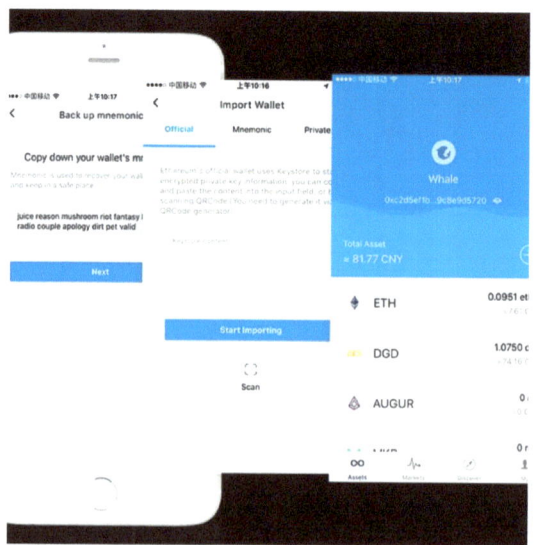

Figure 9: Different screens of the imToken wallet

This is a mobile wallet that is available for Android and iOS users. The wallet supports ETH and ERC20 tokens only. imToken is usually developed in iterations, currently at imToken 2.0. Each version or iteration comes with more advanced features touching on security, user experience and user education. Like many other Ethereum-based wallets, imToken allows users to pay transaction fees according to the speed at which they want their transactions to be processed. Higher fees (referred to as gas prices) leads to faster transactions.

Setting up an imToken wallet is fairly simple. There are no personal details collected, a user just creates a Private key and a password for the wallet. imToken gives users the option to store their keys using keystore. The main hallenge with the wallet is its narrow scope of support for only tokens. Many other wallets will support at least one coin. However, it is ideal for users that want a wallet specifically meant for handling tokens.

Chapter 4: Web wallets

Web wallets are also known as online wallets. They run on web browsers, just like normal websites do. However, the list of options for web wallets is limited. This is due to the security fears that there are very many threats that can take advantage of the vulnerabilities in web-based operations to steal a user's funds. These wallets are therefore commonly used to hold just a few coins or are paired with hardware wallets where users can swiftly send their funds to just after completing their transactions. Therefore, users should be highly cautious with web wallets. The following are the commonly used online wallets:

4.1. GreenAddress

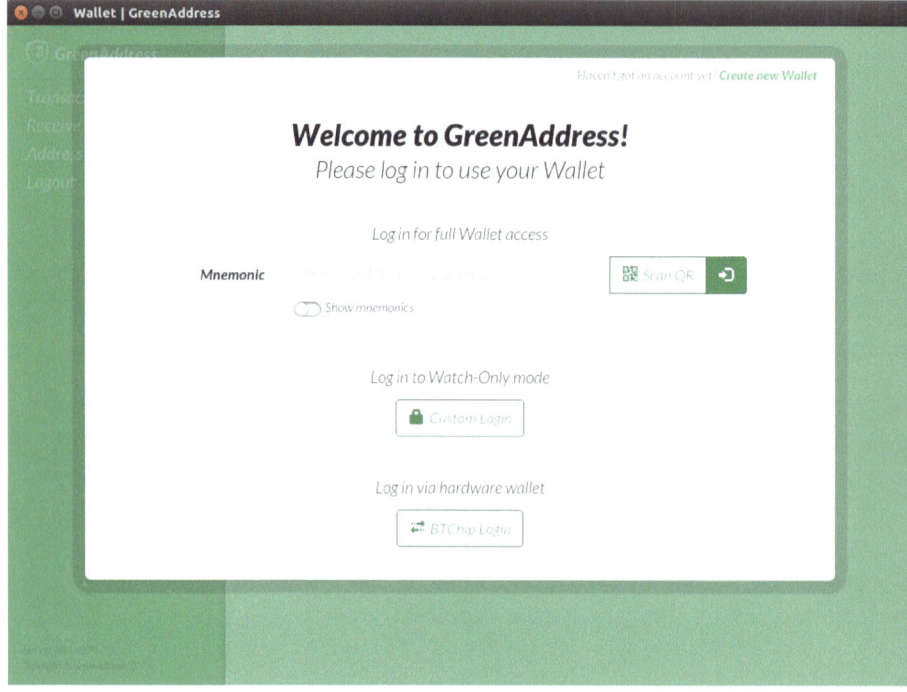

Figure 10: GreenAddress interface

GreenAddress is a Bitcoin wallet. This is a wallet that was developed with the risky environment of browsers in mind. GreenAddress, therefore, comes with several features meant to prevent a user's wallet from being attacked by hackers and malware. The wallet supports multi-signature which means, a transaction can only be completed when a second user approves of it. Therefore, even if hackers gain access to a GreenAddress wallet, there is nothing that they can do since transactions will have to be authorized by another party. GreenAddress also supports hardware wallets and this is highly convenient for users that want to hold lots of cryptocurrencies. The wallet can help the user to quickly move the funds to the hardware wallet.

2-factor authentication is also supported by the wallet. This makes it harder for any hacker to have access to the wallet in the first place as they would need to have more than just the user's password. GreenAddress also incorporates a feature called watch-only. This is a method of access the wallet only to view balances or transactions. This can be done on public WiFi as there is no exchange of credentials that could be captured by malicious parties sitting on the public WiFi network. GreenAddress assures its users that they are in complete control of their funds. There is a feature called nLockTime which is a presigned transaction that will automatically release a user's funds upon expiry. Therefore, even if GreenAddress was to disappear, a user will still get back their funds at the end of the nLockTime.

4.2. BitGo

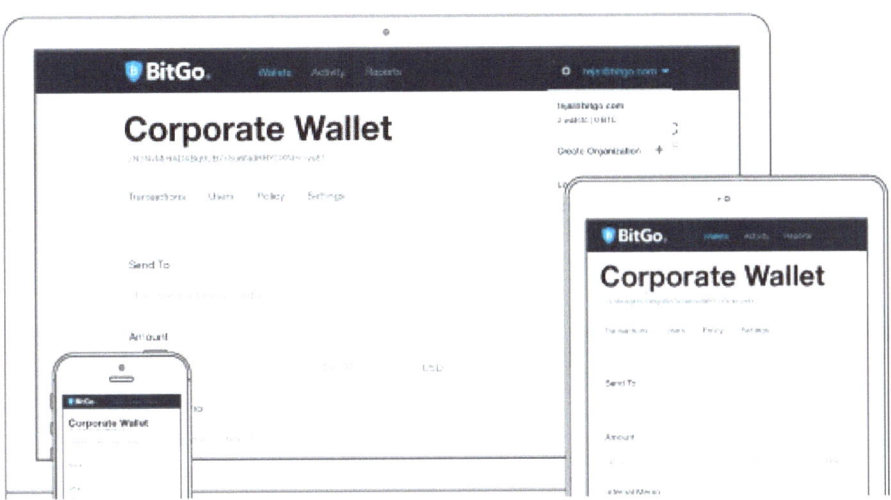

Figure 11: BitGo wallet on mobile, app and laptop

BitGo is a wallet that supports Bitcoin, Bitcoin Cash, Bitcoin Gold, Ripple, LiteCoin, and Ethereum. It is a trusted web wallet especially by the owners of Bitcoin. The wallet currently processes over $1 billion in transactions each month and this is a show that it is a trusted platform. Bitcoins are highly targeted by cyber attackers on the internet. Therefore, the best way to deal with such a risky environment is to only use the reputable platforms to hold the cryptocurrency. BitGo supports multi-sig where two or three Private keys are generated. At least BitGo and the wallet owner must have a key and optionally, a third user can be added to have the third key. With every transaction, these parties must be involved. Therefore, a hacker will not be able to make a transaction because they cannot get these parties to participate. In addition to this, the wallet support 2-factor authentication whereby one has to successfully authorize themselves using two methods to be given access to the wallet.

BitGo has an enterprise version that offers corporate clients even more security to help them with their cryptocurrency assets. Its customers are big names in the cryptocurrency industry such as Kraken and Bitstamp. The level of trust that these big companies have in BitGo shows that is a reliable platform. The major concern with BitGo is that it is centralized hence a user's Private keys are stored by a third party. However, the user encrypts them with a password to ensure their security.

4.3. Blockchain.info

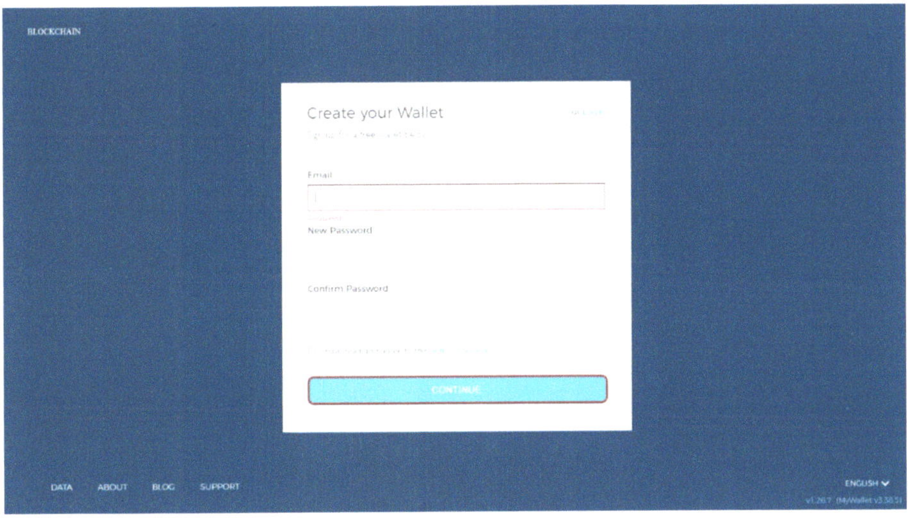

Figure 12: Blockchain.info interface

Blockchain.info is one of the most popular wallets used by cryptocurrency owners. Blockchain.info has transacted over $200 billion worth cryptocurrencies and currently hosts 26 million wallets and this shows that it is a trusted wallet. The wallet also claims to offer the lowest transaction fees and is accessible in over 140 countries. It supports Bitcoin and Ethereum. Apart from being a wallet, Blockchain.info is a platform that offers developers real-time data about the crypto world for analysis. Blockchain.info also supports the direct exchange of Bitcoin and Ether without the user having to leave the platform. It is also used for buying and selling Bitcoin. The wallet is intuitive making it easy to use for new users since it does get a lot of new users that wish to buy coins for the first time. The wallet uses common security approaches; 2-factor authentication and a backup seed. These have been explained in depth in previous sections. The 2-factor authentication makes it hard for hackers to gain access of one's account and the backup phrase or seed enables a user to recover their funds at any time should they lose their wallet ID or password. The main challenge with this wallet is that it is centralized. Therefore, if it goes down, there is a possibility that some users on the platform will lose their cryptocurrencies.

4.4. MyEtherWallet

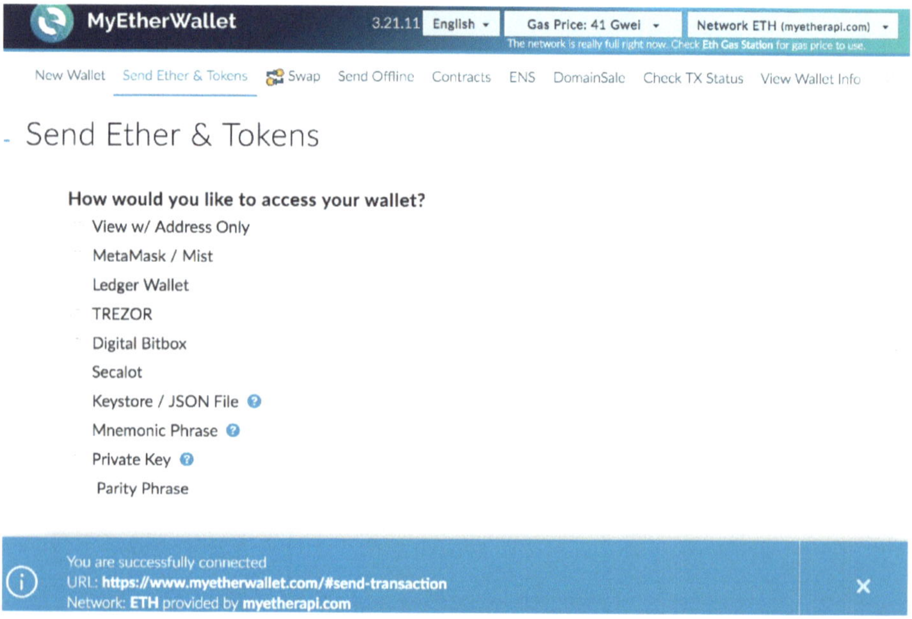

Figure 13: MyEtherWallet interface

This is a wallet that only supports Ethereum and ERC20 tokens. It is open source client-side tool that allows the user to interact with the Ethereum Blockchain from their app. The app is available for both iOS and Android devices. MyEtherWallet is also compatible with many other wallets. These include Jaxx, Mist, MetaMask , Trezor and Ledger Nano S. This allows a user unparalleled flexibility to move around funds over several platforms. However, MyEtherWallet is lacking in terms of features when compared to similar apps. It does not include a mechanism for buying, selling or converting cryptocurrencies.

Therefore, one has to use external platforms such as Coinbase and ShapeShift. However, the wallet allows one to send their Ethereum coins or ERC20 tokens. The beauty of Ethereum is that one can choose the amount of money to pay for transaction fees depending on how soon they want it to be completed. Therefore, its flexibility in terms of being integrated with other wallets and ability to choose the fees and speed of transactions make MyEtherWallet a recognizable web wallet.

4.5. MetaMask

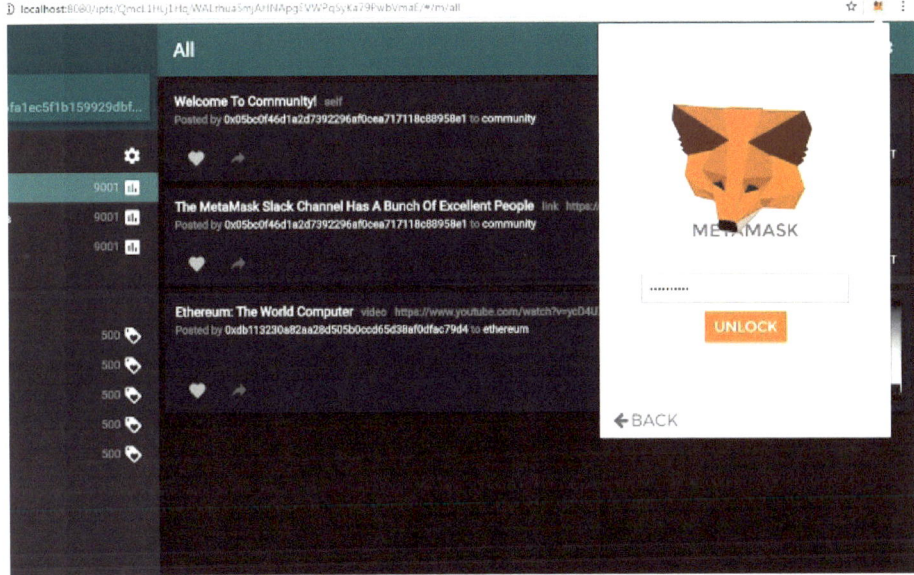

Figure 14: MetaMask web wallet

MetaMask is a wallet with more capabilities than just holding cryptocurrencies. It is a web-based Ethereum wallet that can be accessed using Firefox, Opera and Chrome extensions. The extension turns a browser into an

Ethereum browser. This allows the user to run access the Ethereum Blockchain directly from the browser.

Once you are signed up on MetaMask, the advantages of having an Ethereum browser start to unfold. One can view balances on EtherScan. Etherscan is a BlockExplorer that allows one to look around the entire Ethereum Blockchain and find prices, look for transactions and prices among other pieces of information. Through Etherscan, you can also build decentralized apps (dApps). MetaMask allows for a user to run dApps on their browsers as well. In addition to this, MetaMask comes with Coinbase and ShapeShift. Coinbase is ideal for converting between fiat and cryptocurrency while ShapeShift is for converting between cryptocurrencies. MetaMask is a commonly used wallet by the niche of users that are involved in ERC20 tokens and ICOs. If one has been in an ICO and received some ERC20 tokens, they can be added to MetaMask. However, MetaMask cannot send tokens but will direct those who wish to do so to MyEtherWallet.

The disadvantage of this wallet is tied to the fact that it is a web-based wallet. Therefore, it is possible for other sites or cookies stored on the browser to know that you are signed into the wallet. This is a privacy fear and the wallet usually tells its users to sign off MetaMask once they are done using it.

Chapter 5: Hardware wallets

These are highly secured devices that are offline thus keep Private keys in safe cold storage where they cannot be stolen. Even when connected to the internet, a user's Private key remains safely stored in the wallet. Unlike most other wallets that are free, hardware wallets are purchased as one would buy any other electronic device. Hardware wallets have several advantages over other types of wallets. They never expose a user's Private key even to the user's computer, they are immune from viruses, are heavily encrypted and will normally host multiple cryptocurrencies. Their downside is that they cost money. Hardware wallets are mostly used by users that have security fears, and many users are adopting them due to the increased number of cyber attacks globally. Hardware wallets often have the same features. The following is a list of some of the commonly used hardware wallets:

5.1. Trezor

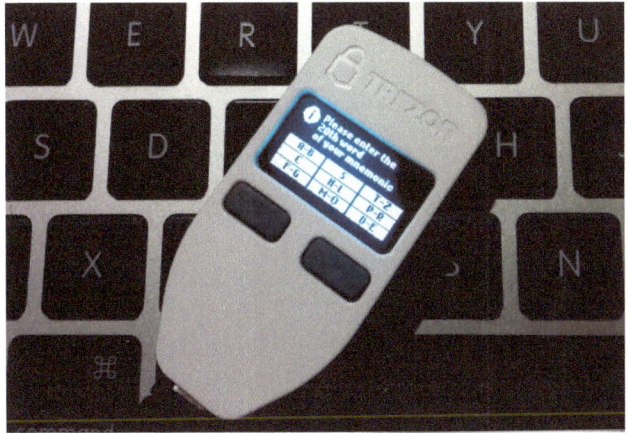

Figure 15: Trezor wallet

This is a famous Bitcoin wallet since it was the first Bitcoin hardware wallet. This wallet gives the reliable safety features of cold storage yet the convenience levels matching those of a hot wallet. Trezor costs $99. For this price, the wallet offers several top-notch security features that justify the cost. The hardware itself is a device that has a display window and comes with a USB connector. The device has been made to be water-proof, fire-proof, shock-proof and hacker-proof. The device comes with two hardware buttons and one must press them at the same time to complete a transaction.

Trezor gives the user complete control of their Private keys but in a very secure environment. These keys can be backed up through a backup phrase and a user is normally guided through this as they configure the wallet for first-time use. The wallet will generate a 24-word seed to be used as a backup. The generation of the phrase is done offline because it is of high significance to the security of the wallet. This seed is what can be used to recover one's wallet. As an added form of security, a user can include a password for this seed.

Access to the Trezor wallet is via PIN. When one enters an incorrect PIN, they have to wait for an increasing period of time. Entering the PIN 30 times translates to a waiting period of 17 years before one can try the 31st time. The Trezor wallet normally interfaces with a web wallet called myTrezor.com to enable to do transactions. The web wallet is normally the interface through which the wallet can be used. Other web wallets are including support for Trezor as well. Therefore, it is possible to make transactions through third-party web wallets with Trezor. The wallet has not had any issues so far and is one of the highly respected wallets in the industry.

5.2. Ledger Nano S

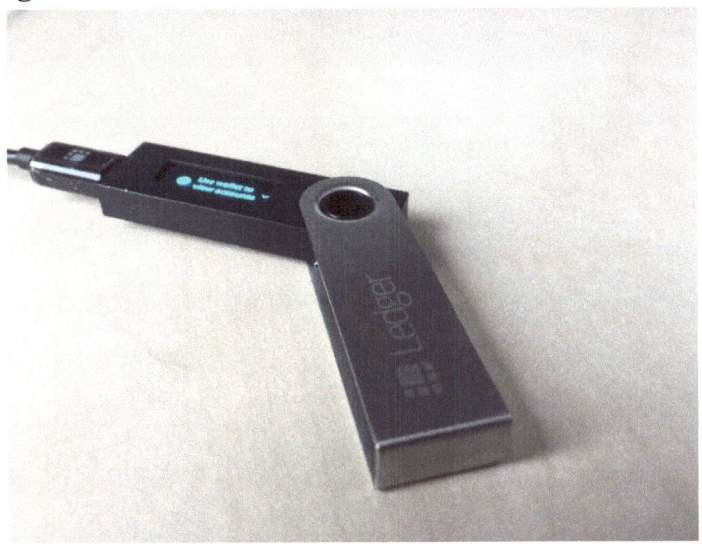

Figure 16: Nano Ledger S wallet

Ledger Nano S shares the same features as Trezor. It has a small display and two physical buttons used to confirm transactions. The setup process is also similar. One is required to set up a PIN and then a 24-word phrase is generated to be used for backup purposes. In addition to this, Ledger Nano plans to add a passphrase to this generated 24-word phrase to make it even harder for any hacker to recover a Ledger Nano wallet. Ledger Nano costs about 79 euros or $92. Ledger Nano can be accessed through the Ledger Manager app that a user is directed to download and install on their computer.

Other hardware wallets such as Keepkey include almost the same features as Trezor and Ledger Nano S. In summary, they are the most secure wallets, they require hardware inputs to confirm transactions and keep a user's Private key offline on cold storage. They can hardly be hacked and are very safe to use even on public network connections.

Chapter 6: Paper wallets

Paper wallets are safe ways of storing cryptocurrencies in a method that is devoid of electronics, software, mobile apps or web apps. Paper wallets are completely offline and a cold storage for Private keys. One has complete control over a paper wallet and is not concerned with the issues such as hackers or malware. Paper wallets are used in rare circumstances by those that understand the technicalities behind setting the wallets up and also when one wants to just stash cryptocurrencies for a long period of time. The disadvantages of paper wallets are many and this makes them less than ideal storage methods. They can be stolen by people that have access to them, as long as they can take a picture of the paper wallet. They are also fragile. They will get worn out with time and are also at risk of fire and water damage. The type of ink used to print the paper might also affect their durability as some types of inks will fade away over time. They can also be lost easily or the owner might forget where he or she kept the paper. Nevertheless, they are still used by enthusiasts.

There are online generators of paper wallets that can be accessed from a browser. This is the riskiest bit and one has to ensure that the computer they are using is free of any malware. The user then has to visit the paper wallet generator pages such as WalletGenerator.net. They will be able to download a zip file containing the contents that enable the wallet generation. The content will include an HTML file. Before opening it, all connections to the computer must be turned off, WiFi, LAN, Bluetooth and any other type of connection. When one opens the HTML file, it will open in a browser with a page to generate the wallet. One is advised to manually type in a certain number of random characters or hover a mouse to set a seed.

When the HTML file has the number of characters it needs, it begins the wallet generation. A new page will come up and it will have a set of two keys and QR codes will be displayed. These can be printed off and photocopied by the user. After this, the page generated should be deleted. The printed public address can be used to store cryptocurrencies while the Private key can be used to authorize transactions. The Private key must be kept secret and from the view of anyone else apart from the owner. Nevertheless, these wallets are highly technical, face many other risks and not very convenient for regular users.

Conclusion

This book has gone through the different types of cryptocurrency wallets available today. It has explained how cryptocurrency wallets work and the differences between a wallet and an exchange. It has talked about desktop wallets, given their advantages and disadvantages and analyzed some of the most commonly used desktop wallets. It has also looked into mobile wallets and explained their convenience. The commonly used mobile wallets have been analyzed and their pros and cons evaluated.

Web wallets have also been discussed as well, the nature of the risky environment they operate in has been discussed and the most commonly used web wallets have been explained as well as the features they include to make them secure. The book has then talked about hardware wallets, some of the most secure wallets. In the analysis, the similarity in the security features of different hardware wallets has been explained and the reasons why they are the safest ways of storing cryptocurrencies has been explained.

Lastly, the book has looked into paper wallets and gone through the setup procedure of one. In its analysis, the book has given out the challenges of paper wallets that make them less-than-ideal methods of keeping cryptocurrencies. Depending on your preferences, this book has given the full range of options that you have when it comes to storing your cryptocurrencies. From the assessment of all these wallets, you will find that hardware wallets are safe but costly, mobile wallets are convenient for use on the go, web wallets are ideal for online transactions, desktop wallets are safer alternatives for online wallets and paper wallets are good for long-term offline storage.

Acknowledgement

- Jo-Yu Duh
- Wei-Shiun Chen

www.ingramcontent.com/pod-product-compliance
Lightning Source LLC
Chambersburg PA
CBHW040332220526
45473CB00009B/2658